THE PRAYER OF OBEDIENCE

BOOK 1

SUPERNATURAL GROWTH SERIES

THE PRAYER OF OBEDIENCE

CAUSING SUPERNATURAL GROWTH

BY
DR STUART ROBINSON

Author of the best selling book *Mosques & Miracles*

Published by
CityHarvest Publications
PO Box 6462
Upper Mt Gravatt QLD 4122, Australia

www.cityharvest.org.au
chp@cityharvest.org.au

The Prayer of Obedience
Copyright © 2005 by Stuart Robinson

ISBN: 0-9577905-7-0

Scripture quotations in this publication are from the *Holy Bible*, New International Version (NIV). Copyright © 1973, 1978, 1984 International Bible Society, Zondervan Bible Publishers. All rights reserved.

Originally published 1992 with third edition published in 2003 as *Praying The Price (ISBN: 064610948-0)*. Revised and updated with two new chapters and a new title 2005.

All rights reserved under International Copyright Law. Contents and/or cover may not be reproduced in whole or in part except for brief quotations, reviews or articles, without the express written consent of the publisher.

Printed in Australia.

About this Book

Perhaps the most profound request Jesus' disciples ever made was, *"Lord, teach us to pray"* (Luke 11:1). They saw Him praying and they also noted the supernatural power which radiated throughout His ministry. They made the connection and implemented it in the early years of the founding of the church. In fact *"they devoted themselves…to prayer"* (Acts 2:42; Colossians 4:2).

In the West we are time scarce because we have crowded our lives with so many other activities—and we are paying a heavy price for it. Western church is in decline. Into the spiritual vacuum left in its wake other non-Christian religions are rushing. But prayer by itself is seldom enough to release supernatural power, especially when it comes to growing a church. Wherever one looks throughout history two human activities attract God's attention. When both are present supernatural intervention is often the result. These are prayer and obedience. This is certainly so in the growth of any church.

The book of Acts makes this abundantly clear. History repeats and demonstrates the formula again and again. The Senior Pastor of the world's largest church, David Yonggi Cho, when asked what the secret of their success was, answered, "We just pray and obey."

But all is not lost. If, like the third world church we recapture prayer and obedience and add to them another vital element

– persistence, we may also see spectacular revival as is already happening in those other places.

The purpose of this book is to demonstrate from the Bible and history that whenever these principles are invoked amazing church growth occurs. They are not the only thing which needs attention, but to pray and obey is absolutely foundational. Nothing of any consequence happens without them.

They are desperately needed to arrest the decline of the church in the West and perhaps in your church as well.

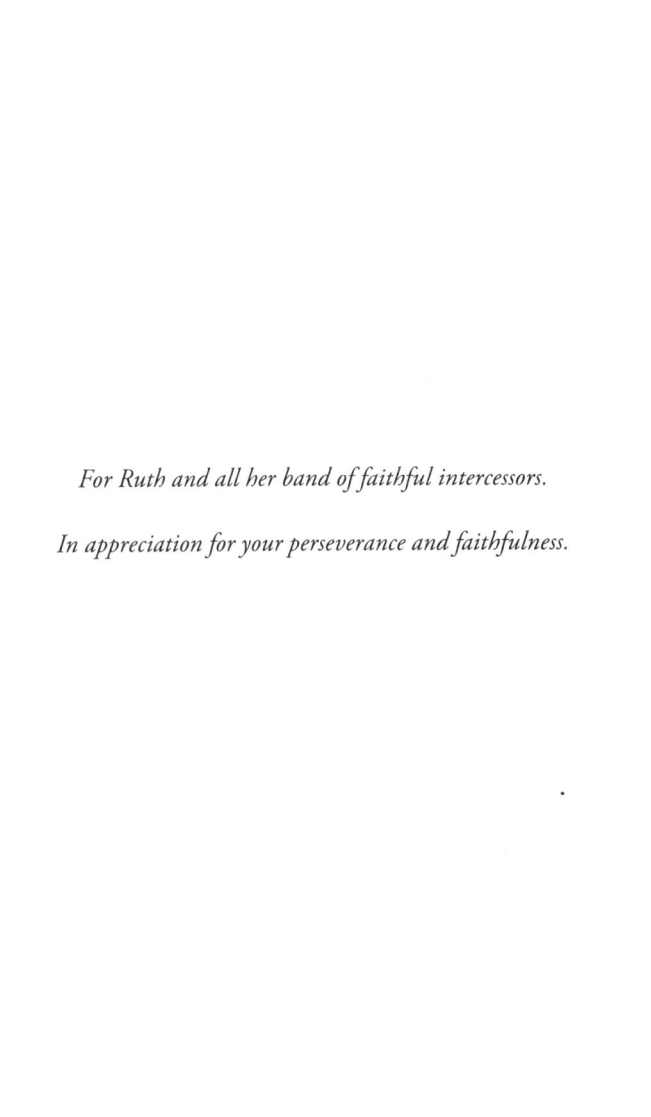

For Ruth and all her band of faithful intercessors.

In appreciation for your perseverance and faithfulness.

"The meaning of prayer is that we get hold of God, not of the answer."

Oswald Chambers

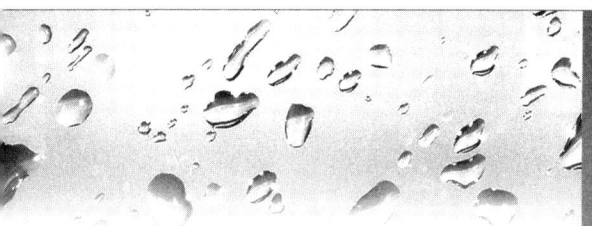

Contents

Pray and Obey 1

Growth - A Supernatural Process 5

Prayer - A Biblical Imperative 7

Extraordinary Prayer In History 9

Challenged to Pray 13

Incredible Social Impact 17

When the Church Prays 19

Persistent Prayer 21

They Never Gave Up 25

Will We "Pray the Price"? 29

Does It Work? 31

So What About You! 35

Pray and Obey

They all joined together constantly in prayer (Acts 1:14)

In 1952 Albert Einstein was asked by a Princeton doctoral student what was left in the world for original dissertation research? Einstein replied, "Find out about prayer."

English preacher Sidlow Baxter, when he was eighty-five years of age, said, "I have pastored only three churches in my more than sixty years of ministry. We had revival in every one. And not one of them came as a result of my preaching. They came as a result of the membership entering into a covenant to pray until revival came. And it did come, every time."[1]

Chaplain of the United States Senate, Richard Halverson, advised that we really don't have any alternatives to prayer. He said, "You can organise until

---

1 Bob J. Willhite, Why Pray? (Altamonte Springs, Florida; Creation House, 1988), 111.

> YOU CAN ORGANISE UNTIL YOU ARE EXHAUSTED. YOU CAN PLAN, PROGRAM AND SUBSIDISE ALL YOUR PLANS. BUT IF YOU FAIL TO PRAY, IT IS A WASTE OF TIME.

you are exhausted. You can plan, program and subsidise all your plans. But if you fail to pray, it is a waste of time. Prayer is not optional. It is mandatory. Not to pray is to disobey God."[2]

Roy Pointer, after extensive research of Baptist churches in the United Kingdom, arrived at the conclusion that wherever there was positive growth, there was one recurring factor: they were all praying churches.

When David Shibley was asked to explain how the church in which he worked as Pastor for prayer grew from 13 to 11,000 people in 9 years he replied, "The evangelistic program of our church is the daily prayer meeting. Every morning, Monday through Friday, we meet at 5.00 a.m. to pray. If we see the harvest of conversions fall off for more than a week, we see that as a spiritual red alert and seek the Lord."[3]

---

2 David Bryant, Concerts of Prayer, (Ventura, California; Regal Books, 1984), 39.

3 David Shibley, Let's Pray in the Harvest, (Rockwall, Texas; Church on the Rock, 1985), 7.

In South Korea the church grew from 1.8% to 40.8% of the population in the twentieth century. Pastor David Yonggi Cho whose church membership exceeded 850,000 attributed its growth as primarily due to ceaseless prayer. In South Korea it is normal for church members to go to bed early so they can arise at 4.00 a.m. to participate in united prayer. It is normal for them to pray all through Friday nights. It is normal to go out to prayer retreats. Cho says that any church might see this sort of phenomenal growth if they are prepared to "pray the price," and to "pray and obey".

> THE EVANGELISTIC PROGRAM OF OUR CHURCH IS THE DAILY PRAYER MEETING. EVERY MORNING, MONDAY THROUGH FRIDAY, WE MEET AT 5.00 A.M. TO PRAY.

One survey showed that pastors in America on average prayed for 22 minutes per day. In Japan it was 44 minutes. In Korea it was 90 minutes. In China it was 120 minutes a day. It is not surprising that the respective growth rates of churches in those countries are directly proportional to the amount of time pastors are spending in prayer.

- *True prayer is a way of life, not just a case of emergency.*
- *Prayerless pews make powerless pulpits.*

GROWTH
- A SUPERNATURAL PROCESS

Only God makes things grow (1 Corinthians 3:7)

The church is a living organism. It is God's creation with Jesus Christ as its head (Colossians 1:18). From Him life flows (John 14:6). We have a responsibility to cooperate with God (1 Corinthians 3:6). We know that unless the Lord builds the house we labour in vain (Psalm 127:1). The transfer of a soul from the kingdom of darkness to that of light is a spiritual, supernatural process (Colossians 1:14).

It is the Father who draws (John 6:44). It is the Holy Spirit who convicts (John 16:8-11). He causes confession to be made (1 Corinthians 12:3). He completes conversion (Titus 3:5). He strengthens and empowers (Ephesians 3:16). He guides into truth (John 16:13). He gives spiritual gifts which promote unity (1 Corinthians 12:25), building up the church (1 Corinthians 14:12), thus avoiding disunity and strife which stunt growth.

> NOTHING THAT MATTERS WILL OCCUR EXCEPT IN ANSWER TO PRAYER....

This is fundamental spiritual truth accepted and believed by all Christians. However, the degree to which we are convinced that all real growth is ultimately a supernatural process and are prepared to act upon that belief, will be directly reflected in the priority that we give to corporate and personal prayer in the life of the church.

It is only when we begin to see that nothing that matters will occur except in answer to prayer, that prayer will become more than an optional program for the faithful few and instead it will become the driving force of our churches. Obviously God wants our pastors, other leaders and His people to recognise that only He can do extra-ordinary things. When we accept that simple premise, we may begin to pray.

✒ *Archimedes said, "Give me a lever and a place to rest it and I will move the world." Prayer moves the hand that moves the universe. Are we leveraging it?*

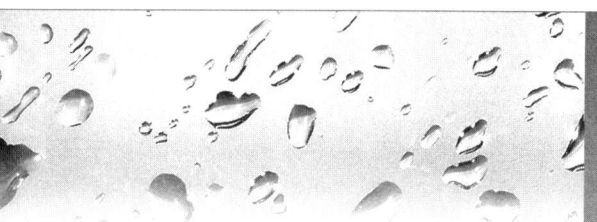

PRAYER
- A BIBLICAL IMPERATIVE

Devote yourselves to prayer (Colossians 4:2)

The battle which Joshua won, as recorded in Exodus 17:8-13, was not so dependent upon what he and his troops were doing down on the plain. It was directly dependent upon Moses' prayerful intercession from on top of a nearby hill, with the support of Aaron and Hur. In the Old Testament, not counting the Psalms, there are 77 explicit references to prayer. The pace quickens in the New Testament.

There are 94 references alone which relate directly to Jesus and prayer. The apostles picked up this theme and practice. So Paul says, *"Pray continually, for this is God's will for you"* (1 Thessalonians 5:16). Peter urges believers to be *"clear minded and self controlled"* so that they can pray (1 Peter 4:7). James declares that prayer is *"powerful and effective"* (James 5:16). John assures us that *"God hears and answers"* (1 John 5:15).

In the book of Acts there are 36 references to the church growing. Fifty eight percent (i.e. 21 of those instances) are within the context of prayer. We would all love to see growth in every church in the world like it was at Pentecost and immediately thereafter. The key to what happened is found in Acts 1:14 where it says: *"They [were] all joined together constantly in prayer."*

> DEVOTE YOURSELVES TO PRAYER. MOST SIGNIFICANT EXPANSION MOVEMENTS OF THE CHURCH THROUGH ITS HISTORY TOOK UP THAT IMPERATIVE.

"They were all joined together" – i.e. of one mind, one purpose, one accord. That is the prerequisite for effectiveness. Then, they were all joined together constantly in prayer. The word used for "constantly" means to be "busily engaged in, to be devoted to, to persist in adhering to a thing, to intently attend to it." It is in the form of a present participle. It means that the practice was continued ceaselessly. The same word and part of speech is used in Acts 2:42(NIV). *"They devoted themselves ... to prayer."* Over in Colossians 4:2(NIV), Paul uses the same word again in the imperative form: *"Devote yourselves to prayer."*

Most significant expansion movements of the church through its history took up that imperative.

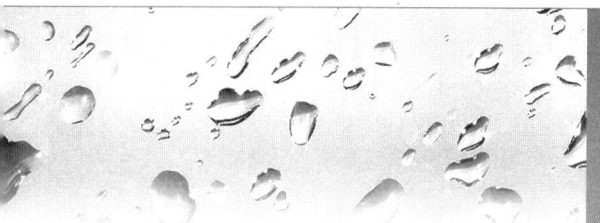

EXTRAORDINARY PRAYER IN HISTORY

The prayer of a righteous man is powerful and effective
(James 5:16)

In 1722 persecuted Moravian Brethren found refuge in Germany under the protection of the Lutheran Christian Count, Nicholas von Zinzendorf. They settled at Hutberg (Watch Hill) and renamed it Herrnhut (the Lord's Watch – Isaiah 62:1, 6-7). In August 1727 the Holy Spirit extraordinarily fell on those gathered in the local parish church. Within two weeks a continuous prayer meeting known as "Hourly Intercession" was established. It proceeded uninterruptedly for 100 years. Through prayer those Moravians were empowered by God. He gave them a passion for the lost which caused them to commission more than 100 missionaries for over 50 nations. All this happened nearly a century before William Carey emerged as "the father of modern missions".

When we read the biographies of William Carey, Adoniram Judson, David Livingstone, Hudson Taylor and others like them, the initiating thrust of the work of their lives began in prayer encounters.

About a century ago, John R. Mott led an extraordinary movement which became known as the Student Christian Movement. It was based among college and university students. It supplied 20,000 career missionaries in the space of 30 years. John Mott said that the source of this amazing awakening lay in united intercessory prayer. It wasn't just that these missionaries were recruited and sent out in prayer. Their work was also sustained through prayer.

Hudson Taylor told a story of a missionary couple who were in charge of ten stations. They wrote to their home secretary confessing their absolute lack of progress. They urged the secretary to find intercessors for each station. After a while, in seven of those locations, opposition melted, spiritual revival broke out and the churches grew strongly. But in three there was no change. When they returned home on their next furlough, the secretary cleared up the mystery. He had succeeded in getting intercessors for only seven of the ten places in China. S. D. Gordon concluded,

"The greatest thing anyone can do for God and man is to pray."[4]

Luther, Calvin, Knox, Latimer, Finney, Moody, all the "greats of God" practised prayer and fasting to enhance ministry effectiveness. John Wesley was so impressed by such precedents that he would not even ordain a person to ministry unless he agreed to fast at least until 4.00 p.m. each Wednesday and Friday.

Yonggi Cho says, "Normally I teach new believers to fast for three days. Once they have become accustomed to three-day fasts, they will be able to fast for a period of seven days. Then they will move to ten-day fasts. Some have even gone for forty days."[5]

These people seem to have latched onto something about which the church in the West hardly knows anything. We are so busy, so active. We try so hard to get something good up and running. But it doesn't seem to grow much or permanently change many

---

4   S. D. Gordon, "Prayer the Greatest Thing," Australia's New Day, April 1983, 40.

5   Paul Y. Cho, Prayer, Key to Revival, WACO, Texas WORD 1984, 103.

lives. Why? Is it that the ground in our countries is too hard? Compared with other times and places, this could hardly be so.

✒ *If you are a stranger to prayer you are a stranger to power.*
✒ *"None can believe how powerful prayer is and what it is able to effect, except those who have learned it by experience." – Martin Luther*

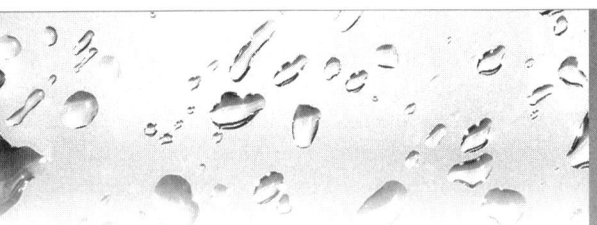

CHALLENGED TO PRAY

I urge then first of all, that requests, prayers, intercession and thanksgiving be made for everyone (1 Timothy 2:1-2)

Back in the 18th century things didn't look good. France was working through its bloody revolution, as terroristic as any of our modern era. America had declared its Rights of Man in 1776. Voltaire was preaching that the church was only a system of oppression for the human spirit. Karl Marx would later agree. A new morality had arisen. Among both sexes in all ranks of society, Christianity was held in almost universal contempt. Demonic forces seemed to have been unleashed to drive the church out of existence. In many places it was almost down and out. Preachers and people were being pelted with stones and coal in places in England if they dared to testify to Jesus Christ in public. But even before those satanic forces collaborated to confound and confuse, it appears that the Holy Spirit had prepared His defense, like a plot out of some "Left Behind" novel.

In the 1740's, John Erskine of Edinburgh published a pamphlet encouraging people to pray for Scotland and elsewhere. Over in America, the challenge was picked up by Jonathan Edwards, who wrote a treatise called, "A Humble Attempt to Promote Explicit Agreement and Visible Union of God's People in Extra-ordinary Prayer for the Revival of Religion and the Advancement of Christ's Kingdom."

For 40 years, through voluminous correspondence around the world, John Erskine orchestrated what became a Concert of Prayer. In the face of apparent social, political and moral deterioration, he persisted. And then the Lord of the universe stepped in and took over. On Christmas Eve 1781, at St Just Church in Cornwall, at 3.00 p.m., intercessors met to sing and pray. The heavens opened at last and they knew it. They prayed through until 9.00 a.m. and regathered on Christmas evening. Throughout January and February, the movement spread and continued. By March 1782 they were praying until midnight. No significant preachers were involved – just people praying and the Holy Spirit responding.

Two years later in 1784, when 83 year old John Wesley visited that area, he wrote, "this country is all on fire and the flame is spreading from village to village."

And spread it did. The chapel which George Whitfield had built decades previously in Tottenham Court Road had to be enlarged to seat 5,000 people – the largest in the world at that time. Baptist churches in North Hampton, Leicester and the Midlands, set aside regular nights devoted to the drumbeat of prayer for revival. Methodists and Anglicans joined in.

> WHEN GOD INTENDS GREAT MERCY FOR HIS PEOPLE, HE FIRST SETS THEM PRAYING.

Matthew Henry wrote, "When God intends great mercy for His people, He first sets them praying."

Across the country prayer meetings were networking for revival. A passion for evangelism arose. Converts were being won – not through the regular services of the churches, but at the prayer meetings! Some were held at 5.00 a.m., some at midnight. Some pre-Christians were drawn by dreams and visions. Some came to scoff but were thrown to the ground under the power of the Holy Spirit. Sometimes there was noise and confusion; sometimes stillness and solemnity. But always there was that ceaseless outpouring of the Holy Spirit. Whole denominations doubled, tripled and quadrupled in the next few years. It swept out from England to Wales, Scotland, the United States, Canada and some Third World countries.

- *He stands best who kneels most.*
- *Satan trembles when he sees the weakest Christian on his knees.*
- *When it is hardest to pray is the time to pray hardest.*

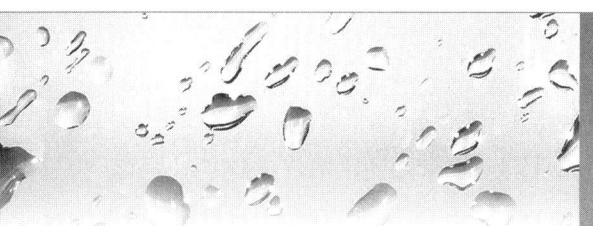

INCREDIBLE SOCIAL IMPACT

I will hear from heaven, forgive and heal (your) land
(2 Chronicles 7:14)

The social impact of reformed lives was incredible. William Wilberforce, William Pitt, Edmund Bourke and Charles Fox were all touched by this movement. They worked ceaselessly for the abolition of the slave trade which finally happened in 1807. William Buxton worked on for the emancipation of all slaves in the British Empire and saw it happen in 1834. John Howard and Elizabeth Fry gave their lives to reform radically the prison system. Florence Nightingale founded modern nursing.

Ashley Cooper, the seventh Earl of Shaftesbury, came to the rescue of the working poor to end their 16 hour, 7-day-a-week work grind. He worked to stop exploitation of women and children in coal mines and the suffocation of boys as sweeps in chimneys. He established public parks and gymnasia, gardens, public libraries, night schools and choral societies.

The Christian Socialist Movement, which became the British Trade Union movement, was birthed. The Royal Society for the Prevention of Cruelty to Animals was formed to protect animals.

> AMAZING GROWTH IN CHURCHES, AND ASTOUNDING CHANGES IN SOCIETY, CAME ABOUT IN PART BECAUSE FOR 40 YEARS ONE MAN PRAYED AND WORKED…

Amazing growth in churches, and astounding changes in society, came about in part because for 40 years one man prayed and worked, seeing the establishment of thousands of similar meetings, all united in calling on God for revival.

Missionary societies were established. William Carey was one who got swept up in that movement. The environment of his situation was that he was a member of a ministers' revival prayer group which had been meeting for two years in Northampton in 1784-86. It was in 1786 he shared his vision of God's desire to see the heathen won for the Lord. He went on to establish what later became known as the Baptist Missionary society. In 1795 the London Missionary society was formed. In 1796 the Scottish Missionary Society was established and later still the Church Missionary Society of the Anglicans was commenced.

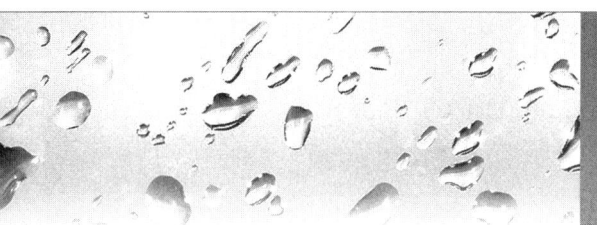

WHEN THE CHURCH PRAYS

If you believe you will receive whatever you ask for in prayer
(Matthew 21:22)

The prayer movement had a tremendous impact, but waned until the middle of the 19th century. Then God started something up in Hamilton, Ontario and the necessity to pray was picked up in New York.

A quiet New York businessman called Jeremiah Lamphier had been appointed by the Dutch Reformed Church as a missionary to the central business district. The church was in decline and the life of the city was somewhat similar. Lamphier didn't know what to do. So he called a prayer meeting in the city to be held at noon each Wednesday. Its first meeting was on September 23, 1857. Eventually, five other men turned up. Two weeks later, they decided to move to a daily schedule of prayer. Within six months, 10,000 men were gathering to pray. The New York newspapers published articles on the revival which had become the city's biggest news. By the spring of 1858,

> 10,000 MEN WERE GATHERING TO PRAY AND THAT MOVEMENT SPREAD ACROSS AMERICA. WITHIN TWO YEARS THERE WERE ONE MILLION NEW BELIEVERS ADDED TO THE CHURCH.

2000 people were meeting in Chicago's Metropolitan Theatre. The movement quickly spread across America. Within two years there were one million new believers added to the church. The movement swept out to touch England, Scotland, Wales and Ulster.

Ireland was a tough place for church. But when news reached Ireland of what was happening in America, James McQuilkan gathered three young men to meet for prayer in the Kells school house on March 14, 1859. They prayed for revival. Within a couple of months a similar prayer meeting was launched in Belfast. By September 21, 20,000 people assembled to pray for the whole of Ireland.

It was later estimated that 100,000 converts resulted directly from these prayer movements in Ireland. It has also been estimated that in the years 1859-60, some 1,150,000 people were added to the church, wherever concerts of prayer were in operation.

PERSISTENT PRAYER

Pray without ceasing (1 Thessalonians 5:17)

Revival in Wales commenced in October 1904. It was spontaneous and was characterised by simultaneous, lengthy prayer meetings. In the first two months, 70,000 people came to the Lord. In 1905 in London alone, the Wesleyan Methodists increased from their base membership of 54,785 by an additional 50,021 people.

In Papua New Guinea the largest single linguistic group is the Enga clans of the Western Highlands. By 1970 their churches were in spiritual decline. To redress the situation people committed to pray. Prayer meetings began with pastors, missionaries and Bible college students joining in. In some villages groups of people agreed to pray daily until God birthed new life in the church. On September 15, 1973, without any prior indication, simultaneously, spontaneously, in village after village as pastors stood to deliver their normal Sunday morning messages, the Holy Spirit descended bringing conviction, confession, repentance and revival.

Normal work stopped as people in their thousands hurried to special meetings. Prayer groups met daily, morning and evening. Thousands of Christians were restored and thousands of people were converted. Whole villages became 100% Christian as the church grew not only in size, but in maturity.

In Cuba in 1990, an Assemblies of God pastor whose congregation never exceeded 100 people meeting once a week, suddenly found himself conducting 12 services per day for 7,000 people. They started queuing at 2.00 a.m. and even broke down the doors just to get into the prayer meetings. Asked to explain these phenomena, Cuban Christians said, "It has come because we have paid the price. We have suffered for the Gospel and we have prayed for many, many years."[6]

When the Overseas Missionary Society saw that after 25 years of work in India all they could report was 2,000 believers in 25 churches, they adopted a new strategy. In their homelands they recruited 1,000 people committed to pray for the work in India for just 15 minutes per day. Within a few years the church

---

6   Greg O'Connor, "Miracles in Cuba," New Day, May 1990, 7-9.

exploded to 73,000 members in 550 churches.

Although the specifics remain unclear, one of the most remarkable increases in church growth anywhere in the history of the church may have been going on for the last half century in China. At the time of the declaration of the People's Republic of China in 1949, Christians were numbered between 700,000 to 1 million. In June 1993 the State Statistics Bureau Report officially declared that there were 63 million Protestant and 12 million Catholic Christians in China. By the turn of the century unofficial estimates put the figure as high as 100 million. This has occurred without outside assistance apart from prayer. David Wang concluded that the key to the phenomenal growth of the church in China is their fervent prayer. He said that through prayer, God "is not their last resort. He is their first and only resort."[7]

> …KEY TO THE PHENOMENAL GROWTH OF THE CHURCH IN CHINA IS THEIR FERVENT PRAYER … THAT THROUGH PRAYER, GOD "IS NOT THEIR LAST RESORT. HE IS THEIR FIRST AND ONLY RESORT."

---

7   David Wang, "And they Continued Steadfastly. Part II," Asian Report, September/October 1993, 20.

Wherever that principle of persistent prayer is invoked, amazing things happen. In 1982 Christians in East Germany started to form small groups of ten to twelve persons, committed to meet to pray for peace. By October 1989, 50,000 people were involved in Monday night prayer meetings. In 1990, when those praying people moved quietly into the streets, their numbers quickly swelled to 300,000 and "the (Berlin) wall came tumbling down."

- *Prayer is a shield to the soul, a delight to God, and a scourge to Satan.*
- *Prayer is a powerful thing; God has bound and tied it to Himself.*
- *Nothing is beyond the reach of prayer except that which lies outside the will of God.*

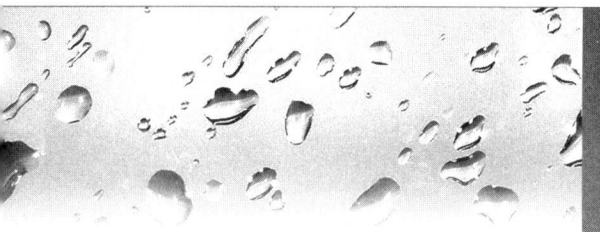

THEY NEVER GAVE UP

Be joyful in hope, patient in affliction, faithful in prayer
(Romans 12:2)

As an early missionary to the Fijian Islands was dying he prayed, "Lord, save Fiji, save Fiji; save these people, O Lord; have mercy upon Fiji. Save Fiji."[8] In the twenty-first century that prayer is being dramatically answered. The President, Prime Minister and Senior Government officials have become committed Christians and have led the way in dedicating the nation to God. Tribes are being reconciled. Millions of dollars worth of marijuana plants have been voluntarily destroyed by farmers. Witch doctors have burned artifacts and made public confessions at church services. Many reports also refer to the regeneration of coral reefs, marine stocks, a new abundance of fruit and other crops the like of which has not been seen for decades. In analyzing what has caused the change, Ian Shelton concludes that the number one factor was

---

8 *The Evangelical Methodist*, n.d..

that "key leaders faithfully interceded for their nation for twenty years….(through) hardship and poverty…. they never gave up."[9]

By early 1995 churches in Cali, Columbia realized their city was being overrun by drug barons, their illicit money and its byproducts of corruption, bribery, violence, prostitution and other evils. Evangelical churches called for a public prayer meeting and in March 1995, 20,000 people gathered to pray. In August of that year 40,000 came. In December 45,000 gathered.

On the weekend of the first gathering the daily rate of homicides fell from 15 to zero. Within nine months six of the seven drug barons fell. 5,000 people accepted Jesus at each major gathering. Then in December 1995 Pastor Julio Ruibal was assassinated. Later the Roman Catholic archbishop of Cali was murdered. Ten other bishops, over 50 priests and more than 100 pastors were also threatened.

Pastor Ruibal's wife, Ruth said, "No price is too high… Even though there may be difficult days ahead… We

---

9 Ian Shelton, "What we can learn from Fiji revival," *One heart for the nation*, Oct – Dec 2004, 3.

don't want to settle for anything less than His presence in Columbia."[10]

On March 24, 2005, 50,000 people filled the Cali stadium for the twenty-sixth time for united prayer. 95 other cities, towns and villages across Columbia joined in. Cali's mayor said his goal was that the displaced people of his region find their "true home in Christ". Newspapers later reported that homicides had dropped by 60.9% during the week.[11]

In the San Salvadoran suburb of San Marcos, drug dealing, bars, occult practices and gang warfare had earned it the reputation of being the nation's most violent area. Legitimate businesses were closing down. Finally when dengue fever struck, pastors mobilized their people to clean up the area. For three months they fasted and prayed. Within a year the national police declared the area free of violence. "Banks reopened, cash machines reappeared on the streets, 14 notorious bars closed…drug activity disappeared….the Mayor and the Secretary of Health became born-again Christians along with a number of their assistants."[12]

---

10   Inger J. Logelin, "It's just not the same in Cali, Columbia", www.sentinelgroup.org

11   "Transformation Continues in Cali," OpenHeaven.com 23/04/2005.

12   Barni Feuerhaken, Gospel frees a city from gangs, drugs, witchcraft. Dawn Report, September 2002, 1-2

This is spiritual warfare and its side effects.

> A SPIRITUAL HIGHWAY WAS BEING FORMED AS MORE THAN 22 MILLION PEOPLE PRAYED TOGETHER...

On March 12, 2001, 45,000 people gathered in a stadium in Capetown to pray. In 2002, the movement spread to incorporate the provinces of South Africa in eight stadiums with 350,000 people praying. In 2003, 2.5 million people in 130 stadiums in 27 sub-Saharan nations joined in a day of simultaneous prayer. By May 2, 2004, the prayer movement blazed even brighter to incorporate the 56 nations of Africa rallying in more than 2,000 sites. A spiritual highway was being formed as more than 22 million people prayed together for the Transformation of Africa. This was the largest prayer meeting in recorded history. In 2005 on May 15 many other nations of the world joined in. Prayer is at last again on the agenda of the church. The question is will we persist or will we allow ourselves to be distracted again.

- *To look around is to be distressed.*
- *To look within is to be depressed.*
- *To look up is to be blessed.*

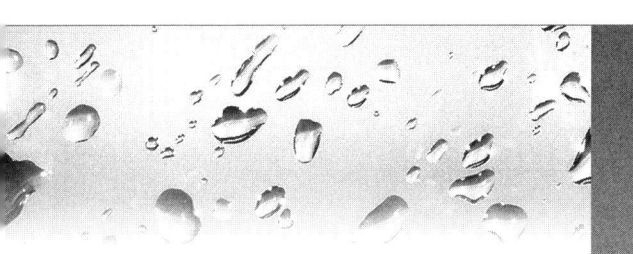

Will We "Pray the Price"?

*By prayer and petition with thanksgiving,
present your requests to God (Philippians 4:6)*

Today there is great pressure from many directions in our society to work harder, to become smarter, to produce results, or to be moved aside. The church in many countries is in danger of absorbing this mentality into its own attitudes and practices, forgetting that in the divine-human endeavour, success comes not by might nor by power, but by a gracious release of God's Holy Spirit (Zechariah 4:6).

Years ago, R. A. Torrey said, "We live in a day characterised by the multiplication of man's machinery and the diminution of God's power. The great cry of our day is work, work, work! Organise, organise, organise! Give us some new methods! Devise some

> THE GREAT NEED OF OUR DAY IS PRAYER, MORE PRAYER AND BETTER PRAYER.

new machinery! But the great need of our day is prayer, more prayer and better prayer."[13]

In much of the church we now have the most up to date state of the art technology available to communicate the Gospel. Yet comparatively little seems to be happening in so many countries. In terms of growth and mission, could it be that while the world has learned to communicate with robots on Mars, in sections of the church we have forgotten to communicate with the Lord of the Earth?

If that is so, then our best course of action is to join the first disciples to ask the Head of the church, "Lord, teach us to pray" (Luke 11:1).

- *"I have so much to do (today) that I shall spend the first three hours in prayer." – Martin Luther*
- *"Prayer is the Christian's most glorious privilege, most enlarging opportunity and most essential obligation; for it opens the doors of communication with God, makes easier our access to others and gives us the surest way to bring people to a saving knowledge of Christ." – Billy Graham*

---

13 R. A. Torrey, The Power of Prayer (Grand Rapids, Michigan; Zondervan, 1974), 190.

DOES IT WORK?

My house will be called a house of prayer (Mark 11:17)

In September 1995 the church, in which I work, Crossway, came into being on a new 2.2 hectare (6 acres) site accommodating several hundred people in eastern suburban Melbourne.

By 2005:

- Attendances at weekend services averaged 3500.

- Additional land had been purchased to increase campus size to 6 hectares (15 acres).

- $20m worth of buildings, equipment, facilities and property had been paid for.

- Four other language congregations, in addition to English were operating on campus.

- Seven other churches had been planted or re-established.

- 54 full time cross-cultural workers were commissioned and significantly supported mostly across the 10/40 window.

- Of those being added to the church each year approximately 10% of total congregational attendance (i.e. 350 in 2005) were first time commitments.

In a nation such as Australia where church attendance has been in decline for decades and Christian influence has been significantly eroded and marginalised, how was this possible?

In our vision statement was embedded our determination to be a "Prayerful People". For a complex organism like church to live and grow continuously, many issues require attention. But none is more important than prayer. Therefore at Crossway:

- There is a prayer department headed by a full time paid pastor for prayer who supervises and co-ordinates all prayer initiatives.

- Every pastor has a team of personal intercessors.

- Every department is supported by their own teams of intercessors which operate especially when that department is ministering.

- At approximately 6.00 a.m. each day specialist prayer teams meet to pray for the church, the city, the nation and wider issues.

- The church's annual September conference is preceded by 30 days of prayer and fasting.

- A 250 seat prayer chapel facility has been constructed, part of which is used exclusively for prayer.

- A goal is in place to join with other world centres for 24/7 continuous prayer for the church, the nations and you!

"Men may spurn our appeals, reject our message, oppose our arguments, despise our persons, but they are helpless against our prayers." – Sidlow Baxter

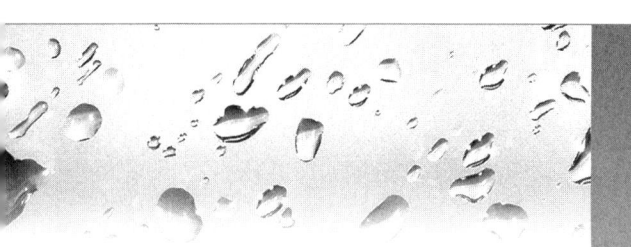

So What About You!

Lord, teach us to pray (Luke 11:1)

Prayer may never happen if we always leave it up to the other person. But the same amazing things which God has done in the past and is doing in various locations today may happen in any church—if you commit to commence and continue.

To avoid prayer becoming self centred and repetitious and to understand what God desires, begin by :

1. Systematically reading your Bible. Soak yourself in it (Deuteronomy 1:8; Matthew 4:4). As you read God's book and start to get His perspective on things, you'll find His book will also read you.

2. Allowing time to think about what the Bible is saying. In our time starved lives, thinking may have become one of our most underutilised abilities.

3. Writing down what you are learning or sensing. That is called journaling. There are many excellent helps available. One very good one is "The Aussie Life Journal," published by CityHarvest Publications. In one diary type book you get a reading plan which guides you through the whole Bible throughout the year and shows you how to record and apply what you are learning. It helps develop your focus towards personal spiritual transformation and in praying for the lost.

4. Applying what you are learning. (Deuteronomy 11:8-32; James 1:22-25).

5. Keeping a list of those things you are bringing to God. Always leave a space beside each item to note His answer whenever it comes.

6. Asking the pastor's permission to start your own prayer group which might ultimately influence the whole of your church's ministry.

For additional help, read "Persevering Prayer," by Stuart Robinson, published by Sovereign World.

A survey of more than 1300 Christian leaders around the world revealed that in their opinion the most important issue for the world wide church is to see established passionate, personal, corporate and consistent prayer.

One of these leaders, Gary Butler of Oklahoma expressed it thus:

"… For today's church to remain strong … it must be a praying church. If we believers … want to see the same mighty move of God that the early church saw we must pray as the early church did."[14]

- *J. Hudson Taylor once said, "Prayer power has never been tried to its full capacity…If we want to see mighty wonders of divine power and grace wrought in the place of weakness, failure and disappointment, let us answer God's standing challenge, 'Call to me and I will answer you and tell you great and unsearchable things you do not know.'" (Jeremiah 33:3)*
- *God is never more than a prayer away. If His church is ever to stand on its feet, it must first sink to its knees.*

---

14 Prayer: No 1 issue in churches, survey of leaders shows, www.bpnews.org, April 12, 2005

Stuart Robinson has been the Senior Pastor of Crossway in Melbourne since 1983. Before that he worked for fourteen years in South Asia where he pioneered church planting among Muslims. He travels extensively as a speaker at Conferences. He is the author of three books including the best selling *Mosques & Miracles*.

He graduated from the Baptist Theological College of Queensland, the University of Queensland, the Melbourne College of Divinity and Fuller Theological Seminary.

Stuart was born in Brisbane and is married to Margaret. They have three married children.